COLONIAL PEOPLE

The Apothecary

CHRISTINE PETERSEN

 **Marshall Cavendish**
Benchmark
New York

Other Marshall Cavendish Offices:

Marshall Cavendish International (Asia) Private Limited, 1 New Industrial Road, Singapore 536196 • Marshall Cavendish International (Thailand) Co Ltd. 253 Asoke, 12th Flr, Sukhumvit 21 Road, Klongtoey Nua, Wattana, Bangkok 10110, Thailand • Marshall Cavendish (Malaysia) Sdn Bhd, Times Subang, Lot 46, Subang Hi-Tech Industrial Park, Batu Tiga, 40000 Shah Alam, Selangor Darul Ehsan, Malaysia

Marshall Cavendish is a trademark of Times Publishing Limited

All websites were available and accurate when this book was sent to press.

Library of Congress Cataloging-in-Publication Data

Petersen, Christine.
The apothecary / by Christine Petersen.
p. cm. — (Colonial People)
Includes bibliographical references and index.
Summary: "Explore the life of a colonial apothecary and his importance to the community, as well as everyday life, responsibilities, and social practices during that time"—Provided by publisher.
ISBN 978-0-7614-4795-5
1.Pharmacists—United States—History—17th century—Juvenile literature. 2. Drugstores—United States—History—17th century—Juvenile literature. 3. United States—History—Colonial period, ca. 1600–1775—Juvenile literature. I. Title.
RS67.U6P48 2011
615'1—dc22
2009015274

Editor: Christine Florie
Publisher: Michelle Bisson
Art Director: Anahid Hamparian
Series Designer: Kay Petronio

Expert Reader: Professor Paul Douglas Newman, Ph.D., Department of History, University of Pittsburgh at Johnstown

Photo research by Marybeth Kavanagh

Cover photo by The Art Archive/Medicine Museum Rome/Gianni Dagli Orti

The photographs in this book are used by permission and through the courtesy of:

Getty Images: 4; MPI, 8; *The Granger Collection*: 12, 15, 17, 41; *The Bridgeman Art Library*: Private Collection, 13; Look and Learn, 20; Bibliotheque des Arts Decoratifs, Paris, France/Archives Charmet, 23; Academie Nationale de Medecine, Paris, France/Archives Charmet, 39; *The Colonial Williamsburg Foundation*: 25, 27, 29, 35; *North Wind Picture Archives*: 37.

Printed in Malaysia (T)
1 3 5 6 4 2

CONTENTS

ONE

Taking a Chance

In the winter of 1606 three small ships set forth from England's capital city of London. They sailed down the Thames River and into the rough waters of the Atlantic Ocean. The ships held a crew of 39 sailors, plus 105 passengers. These men and boys shared one goal: to reach a faraway land called Virginia. They hoped to establish the first permanent English colony in the New World.

It was a long and miserable journey. The ships were tossed by wind and high waves. Virginia seemed like a reward for the passengers' troubles. The three ships arrived in spring, and the settlers found the landscape lush with trees and fruit. The water was full of fish. The colonists chose a spot alongside a river just south of Chesapeake Bay. They quickly constructed a fort, shelters, and a small church. It was also important that they begin farming

Settlers carry lumber toward a
fort and shelters at Jamestown,
Virginia, the first permanent
English settlement in America.

or they might not have enough food to last through the winter. Colonists called their settlement Jamestown, in honor of England's ruler, King James I.

Who Were the Colonists?

These first colonists had very little in common with one another. In England they probably never would have chosen one another's company. But in Jamestown their survival depended on working together. All the men were under contract to the Virginia Company of London. The company paid for their trip and for all the expenses of setting up a colony. In return, colonists were expected to look for gold and make products that could be shipped back for sale in England. Eventually, each man would be given land to farm.

The Virginia Company handpicked people who represented English society. This included gentlemen who came from wealthy families and their personal servants. Most of these gentlemen had never worked, or they had held professional jobs that required no manual labor. Only a few of the early colonists were skilled craftsmen or laborers. There were some soldiers in the group and a few young boys who had probably been orphaned. None of these colonists had any experience in farming. And Jamestown would go a year without any medical assistance. Surgeons Thomas Wotton and William Wilkinson arrived in the spring of 1607. By then almost half of the original colonists had died.

Life and Death in Jamestown

In seventeenth-century England, medical care was broken into clear categories. Physicians spent years training at universities. Their role was to diagnose and treat illnesses. They almost never did the "dirty work" of setting broken bones, pulling teeth, or dressing wounds. These were the job of surgeons. Because a surgeon used his hands (rather than his mind) when working, he was considered a craftsman. The druggist prepared chemicals and herbs to use as medicines. There were no schools for surgeons or druggists. They learned their skills during an apprenticeship. After a year or more of training with an experienced specialist, they could work on their own.

The Virginia Company did not expect illness to be a problem in the new colony. They chose surgeons Wilkinson and Wotton to provide treatment for injuries. They had plenty of opportunities to use their skills in Jamestown. Colonists experienced falls, burns, and other injuries. Some were hurt during battles with the local American-Indian tribes. But the Virginia Company was terribly wrong in its prediction about illness. The main cause of death in

Jamestown was disease. Wilkinson and Wotton had to diagnose illnesses, treat them, and prepare medications. Each man did the work of a physician, surgeon, and druggist.

Colds, bronchitis, and other coughing illnesses claimed many lives. Wilkinson and Wotton also saw cases of influenza. Many colonists suffered from an ailment described as "bloody flux." Also called dysentery, this painful form of diarrhea is caused by drinking water that is contaminated with bacteria or microscopic

The colonists at Jamestown suffered injury and illnesses, half of them dying within the first year of settlement.

parasites. Summer also brought misery, including a mysterious disease that caused fever, chills, headache, and vomiting. Colonists called this disease malaria, from the Latin words for "bad air."

Why Risk the Journey?

It may seem foolish to leave your home and move to a strange land. But the colonists had good reasons for making the journey. England had become a difficult place to live. For centuries common people had been able to farm the land freely. Laws passed in the 1530s split up English land among those who could afford to buy it. Poor citizens had little choice but to move to the cities, which became desperately crowded. Wastes piled up in the streets. Citizens could be imprisoned for sleeping on the street. Formerly wealthy landowners faced prison as well if they could not pay their debts. For all these people the New World offered a fresh start.

The sixteenth century was also a time of religious change in Europe. England had an official religion—the Church of England. People who did not follow that church had to leave England to find religious freedom. Some of these people, called the Pilgrims, came to the New World. They settled England's second New World colony, at Plymouth, Massachusetts, in 1620. Quakers, Catholics, and other religious groups later sought freedom of worship in America as well.

Hanging On

Jamestown slowly overcame its challenges and survived. Within one hundred years thirteen colonies had been established along the Atlantic coast. Most colonists lived in villages and towns. Large farm plantations also became common, especially in southern colonies such as Virginia and South Carolina. And America's first cities were established at this time. By 1700 Philadelphia, New York City, Boston, and Charleston (in South Carolina) were each home to several thousand people.

A city might have several physicians, surgeons, and druggists—all working as specialists, as they had in England. But Jamestown set the real example for medical treatment in the colonies. Most communities had a local expert who could help with any medical problem. This was the apothecary. Colonists called him "Doctor" as they would any physician. Many apothecaries had no certificate to prove their skill. But they were a trusted and important part of the colonial community.

TWO

Meet the Apothecary

Colonists tipped their hats when they passed the apothecary on the street. They greeted him with respect, saying, "How do you do, Doctor? I am right heartily glad to see you." Even if he was busy, the apothecary always stopped to chat. "How does all at home?" he would inquire. This was a polite question among all colonists, but the apothecary asked with extra concern. These were more than his neighbors. Each person in the community might someday be his patient.

Too Many, Too Few

Many apothecaries went to America's growing cities. A colonist named William Davice opened Boston's first apothecary shop in 1646. By the mid–1700s that city had so many apothecaries that they were fighting for customers. Williamsburg was the capital of the colony of Virginia. Its population in 1775 was only about

Colonists in cities such as Boston and Williamsburg had many apothecaries to choose from for their medical needs.

two thousand people, but it had at least six apothecaries. Doctors William Pasteur and John Galt encouraged Williamsburg residents to visit their shop by advertising in the colony newspaper, the *Virginia Gazette*. They advertised that they would try "to keep full and complete Assortments of Drugs and Medicines, which they will endeavor to procure of the very best Quality."

Country villages and plantations had the opposite problem. There were not enough trained apothecaries to work in all of the small villages and widespread towns. A single apothecary might serve an entire county. Plantation owners hired him to come out once or twice a year. These large farms were home to dozens or even hundreds of people: family members, employees, and slaves. The apothecary spent a few days on the plantation, providing a checkup for each person. He refilled the plantation's stocks of medicine and made up plans for treating the sick. He might also wander the countryside, checking in on distant farmers. Since many could not afford his services, these colonists would only call on the apothecary in an emergency.

Outside the cities apothecaries would make house calls, visiting and treating the sick in their own homes.

Anyone Will Do

Some parts of colonial America had no trained apothecary at all. In these places colonists asked their ministers and teachers for medical advice. These men learned about medicine through reading and experience. Common people also had skills that they could use in an emergency. When a tooth was infected, the blacksmith used his tongs to pull it. Farmers grew plants that were useful as medicines. Women played an important role, too. They took care of their families every day. Some became midwives, delivering babies and caring for the new mothers. This was one of the few careers open to women.

Colonists were so desperate for medical help that they would accept it from anyone who called himself "doctor." A confident attitude was enough to get some men started as apothecaries. Trained apothecaries were scornful of these men, calling them "quacks." This opinion was often accurate. Some quacks sold fake medicines to make money and charged outrageous fees. This behavior gave apothecaries a bad reputation. However, some untrained men were sincerely trying to help. They learned how to deal with medical problems and went on to become good apothecaries.

The Apothecary's Day

The apothecary's schedule was demanding. His day was usually divided among many small tasks. There were always medicines to be made. Many of these came from plants grown in the apothecary's own backyard herb garden. House calls were also a regular part of the apothecary's job. The city apothecary visited ill and injured patients throughout his neighborhood. In the countryside, apothecaries traveled long distances on horseback or in horse-drawn carts.

Making medicine was one of the many daily tasks of the apothecary.

The "doctor" was never really off duty. In the evening he read books and newspapers from Europe that contained new ideas about science and medicine. A knock on his door might come at any time, day or night. Sometimes this was a welcome interruption, calling him to deliver a baby. More often it was an emergency. The apothecary did his best to ease the suffering of his critically ill patients. He gave medicines and tried treatments. In some cases his efforts were successful. A patient's fever was reduced or the pain was eased. But late-night visits often ended in sorrow. The apothecary could only comfort the family as they said good-bye to a loved one.

The apothecary was a leader of the community, and so he had other responsibilities that also demanded his time. He might serve as a member of the town council or teach at a local college. He was often involved with the church. Through it all the apothecary also had a home and family to look after. Dr. Hugh Mercer provides an excellent example. Mercer was not only a respected physician and apothecary. He also served as an army officer, fighting alongside George Washington during the French and Indian War in the 1750s. Mercer later settled in the town of Fredericksburg, Virginia. Washington's wife, Martha, became one of his many patients. In 1775 Mercer was called into service once again. He commanded a regiment of soldiers during the Revolutionary War (1775–1783) and lost his life in the effort.

A Second Job

The apothecary rarely made a fortune from his business. Even after a busy day, his cash box might contain only a few coins. In part this was because the apothecary allowed his customers to set up credit accounts. Colonial shopkeepers often offered this option because women and servants did the shopping but never carried money. More commonly the apothecary accepted trade from his patients: food, handmade goods, or services. This barter system worked between colonists. But everyone needed some cash. Many of the apothecary's supplies were very expensive and could be ordered only from England or other countries. His creditors expected to be paid on time, or they would not deliver the goods.

To keep his business going, the apothecary sometimes had to take a second job. In the countryside, farming was a logical choice. The farm provided many products that could be sold: fruits and vegetables, eggs, grains to feed livestock, leather, and wool. It fed his family in hard times. The apothecary could also learn a second profession. Colonial communities often needed more lawyers, judges, or teachers. Another option was to set up a shop. This could be run from the apothecary's home or in a store on a village street. Colonists would drop by the shop even when they were healthy, taking time to enjoy a chat and stock up on supplies.

In order to support their families, some apothecaries took a second job, such as farming.

THREE

The Doctor's Boy

A colonial boy rarely chose his own career. His father decided what job his son would pursue. He also made all of the arrangements for education or training. Apothecaries were admired and respected, so this was a sought-after profession. But there were no medical schools in the American colonies until 1765. Instead, boys had to complete an apprenticeship. They learned by working with a master—an apothecary with years of experience. The apothecary's **apprentice** was usually called the "doctor's boy."

A Virginia apothecary named Dr. William Wills advertised for his ideal apprentice. He preferred a boy "that can write a tolerable hand, can confine himself to the care of an apothecary's shop, and attend some few near the county courts to settle accounts." In other words, he wanted a responsible apprentice who could read, write, and do math. The boy would not get a salary for his work. In fact, the opposite was true: families paid for their sons' apprenticeships.

Most colonists could not afford this fee. For this reason, apothecary apprentices usually came from wealthy families.

Before the apprentice could begin training, he and the **master** signed an **indenture**. This was a kind of contract. The boy promised he would obey the master. He agreed never to tell other apothecaries about the master's patients or medicines. In return, the master promised to tutor "the said Apprentice in the Art and Mystery of an Apothecary." This relationship might last a few months or up to seven years.

Getting to Work

At first the doctor's boy was given all of the most boring jobs in the shop. He swept floors, washed equipment, and made sure the shelves were filled. Any task the master disliked was passed off to the boy as well. He was sent on errands around town and might be asked to collect payments from patients.

As he became familiar with the routine, the apprentice was given more responsibility. The master sent him out to work in the herb garden or to collect plants in the woods. When customers came into the shop, the apprentice sold them medicines and answered their questions. He also began to tag along on house calls, watching everything the master apothecary did.

The apothecary's apprentice spent time reading medical texts and recipes.

Like students everywhere, the apprentice spent a lot of time reading. The master usually had a large library of books. Among these were texts describing the work of Galen (c. 129–199 CE), an early Greek physician. Galen identified four main fluids in the body, calling them "humors." He suggested that illness was caused by an imbalance of the humors. For example, too much of the blood humor was thought to cause fever. The apprentice was taught to relieve the patient's symptoms by increasing the level of another humor called black bile—excrement. The apothecary recommended large meals and gave medications that caused the patient's bowels to move. A third humor, called phlegm, was blamed when the patient had excess nasal mucus. Blankets were packed around the patient, and the person was served glasses of wine. According to the books, this would cause the patient to urinate and sweat. These were the yellow bile humors, and they were taken as evidence that the treatment had worked. The more body fluids produced in response to a treatment, the more successful it was considered.

Other books showed the anatomy of the body or described ways to perform surgery. The herbal was a book of plants. It explained how to identify healing plants and which parts were safe to use. The huge **pharmacopoeia** contained recipes for preparing more complex medicines. These might include ingredients from plants and animals, minerals, and chemicals. Even with a pharmacopoeia in hand, it took years for an apprentice to learn how to prepare all of the medicines correctly.

Trial and Error

Eventually every apprentice needed to practice the real skills of the apothecary: making medicines and treating patients. He began with simple tasks, such as cutting up dried plants. Next he might

The Sweet Smell of Health

Apothecaries understood the need to prevent illness. Patients were encouraged to walk every day and to maintain a hearty diet. Apothecaries gave a variety of medicines to increase health and energy. However, people had no idea that microscopic organisms are a source of disease, so colonial Americans were not concerned about hygiene. They believed that dirt kept out **miasma**, the "unhealthy air" that was thought to cause disease. The apothecary's apprentice was never taught to wash his hands before seeing patients. Surgical instruments were merely wiped off after use.

be asked to use the mortar and pestle. The apprentice held the rod-shaped pestle in his hand and used it to crush or grind ingredients inside the mortar bowl. He could make powders or pastes this way. Accuracy was important when making medicines. The apprentice learned to weigh dry ingredients on scales and to measure liquids in a glass beaker.

There were also many treatments to learn. One of the most common was called bleeding. The apothecary showed his apprentice how to make a careful cut on the patient's arm. The blood drained into a bowl. As much as two pints might be taken at a time. The apprentice also learned to handle leeches. These wormlike animals feed on blood. The apothecary placed them at particular points on the patient's body to reduce swelling and pain.

Moving On

At the end of his contract, a successful apprentice was given a certificate or letter from his master. "I repose my Confidence in his knowledge & Recommend him to all those who require his Skill & Services." These are the words of Dr. Andrew Robertson, a beloved master apothecary who taught many students in colonial Virginia. Robertson and other masters recommended that students go on to study at medical schools in Europe. But few young apothecaries could afford this journey. Most were ready to begin their work in the community.

An apprentice uses a mortar and pestle to prepare medicine.

FOUR

The Apothecary Shop

The colonial apothecary shop was a place filled with curious smells and fascinating objects. Colonists came in and out of the store throughout the day. The apothecary chatted as he filled their orders. Children waited quietly. On a good day they might be given a long piece of black licorice from a glass jar on the counter.

There was much to look at while they waited. Shelves lined the apothecary's walls from floor to ceiling. Colorful pots, vials, and bottles sat along each shelf. They held a variety of glistening oils and strange-looking powders. Racks of drawers and bins were built into the long counter. Some contained familiar items, such as cinnamon and cloves. Others had mysterious labels, such as *Hyssop* and *Cinchona*. One particularly fascinating jar often caught the children's attention. It contained water and a supply of dark, squirming leeches.

The apothecary shop's walls were full of bottles and jars of oils, powders, and herbs.

Selling Sundries

The apothecary made his shop more appealing by selling **sundries** alongside his medicines. In cities with several apothecary shops this variety of products gave him an edge over competitors. In small villages the apothecary shop provided goods that might be available nowhere else.

Customers bought some items that could be used for cooking or health care. These included rhubarb, basil, and honey. Wealthy colonists stocked up on luxury items: coffee, imported black tea, scented soap, and candies. The apothecary also offered cosmetics and clothing dye, needles and thread. Colonists especially appreciated the sundries for dental care. Their teeth were always in terrible condition. It helped when they could buy tooth powders for cleaning and licorice roots for brushing. Colonists even bought files to scrape their teeth clean. Anything was better than facing the apothecary's dental tools.

Making Medicines

Many of the apothecary's medicines contained plant ingredients, so he took care to grow healthy plants. He often began the day by collecting herbs. Some plants had to be cut before the dew dried on them. These would be hung from the ceiling of the shop to dry.

Later, their leaves, flowers, stems, and fruit could be used in medicines. From other plants the apothecary dug up roots and underground stems. Back in the shop he washed these and tossed them into bins for storage.

The apothecary prepared two types of medicines: those to prevent illness and those to treat symptoms. Preventive medicines were called **benefits**. Colonists often came into the shop to stock

Ingredients such as garlic, rose hips, and spearmint could always be found in the apothecary shop.

up on these. Colonists ate garlic as a benefit for digestion. Tea made from sassafras roots was drunk to improve energy. The fruit of rose plants, called rose hips, was also made into tea. The apothecary recommended this benefit to prevent scurvy, a painful disease that caused loose teeth and skin rashes.

Simples and **compounds** were medicines used to treat symptoms. Simples contained only plant ingredients, but they were prepared in many ways: as teas, powders, and syrups. Almost every colonist kept a supply of spearmint in the house. The apothecary cut up the dried leaves of this plant and sold them as a tea to treat stomachache. Horehound tea required a bit more preparation. The apothecary started by soaking the leaves in boiling water for ten minutes or so. Then he poured the tea through a strainer to remove the leaves. A large amount of honey was added. This sweet syrup was sold in bottles. Horehound tea was the colonists' favorite treatment for colds, influenza, and asthma.

The apothecary took out his pharmacopoeia when he wanted to make compound medicines. Some of these recipes were so complex that it took a half day to complete all the steps. An example is the recipe for pills to stop vomiting. The apothecary began by grinding red coral and amber with the mortar and pestle. These hard substances had to be crushed over and over again until they formed a fine powder. Oils of cinnamon and nutmeg were mixed in, along with a strongly scented tree oil called turpentine. This paste was placed on a flat ceramic tile. Apothecary tiles were usually marked with lines for measuring. Using his hands, the apothecary pressed the paste into a long, thin roll. He followed the lines on the tile to cut evenly sized pills from the roll. Finished pills were dried and placed in glass bottles to be sold.

The Consultation Room

Patients often needed medical advice before they could buy medicines. At these times the apothecary turned the shop

The apothecary spent hours preparing medicines.

over to his apprentice. The apothecary and his patients went into a small, private room at the back of the shop. He spent a long time talking to his patients. He asked them to describe their symptoms. Their diet, sleep, and exercise routines were also important to know. The apothecary wrote down information about his patients' bodily functions, such as how often they went to the bathroom. He even checked to make sure they were happy and not too stressed. By comparison, the physical examination was quite brief. He might only take a pulse, check skin color, and ask his patients to cough. This was usually enough information for a **diagnosis**.

The apothecary was ready to do more than prescribe medication. He kept a variety of instruments on hand to provide treatment. He had chisels, files, and pliers for pulling teeth. If a patient needed surgery, he used needles, scissors, knives, and cloth dressings. Fevers and infections were often treated by **bloodletting**—cutting the skin or allowing leeches to suck blood from the patient. But usually a patient with such serious problems could not make it to the shop. In these cases the apothecary packed up his equipment in a wooden chest and rode to make a house call. It might be many hours before he made it back to the shop.

Make a Fruit-and-Spice Pomander

Colonial people reasoned that good smells must be able to ward off disease. Balls of scented material called pomanders were often used for this purpose. Some pomanders were hollow metal balls with space inside to hold scented herbs or oils. Others were made of dried fruit soaked in spices.

Apothecaries carried pomanders as protection when they went to visit patients with contagious diseases. Apothecaries also sold herbs and spices in their shops. Women bought ingredients to make pomanders at home.

We now know that odors cannot cause or prevent disease. Still, pomanders are a pleasant touch in any room. The fruit shrinks over time, but the delightful scent can last for years.

Things You Will Need

powdered spices: cinnamon, nutmeg, allspice, ginger, coriander (choose two or more that you like)

sandalwood oil

a medium-sized orange or lemon (look for fruit with no bruises or breaks in the skin)

a roll of narrow masking tape—no more than 1 inch wide

a small knitting needle or short, clean nail

approximately 1 ounce of whole cloves

one paper lunch bag

colored ribbon (same width as masking tape)

(continued)

Directions

1. Measure out 1 tablespoon of each powdered spice. Use a spoon to mix the spices in a small bowl.

2. Add four drops of sandalwood oil to the spices. (The oil is a preservative—it keeps the fruit from decaying.) Mix the oil and spices, and set aside.

3. Wrap a strip of masking tape around the fruit, starting at the stem. (Later you will put a ribbon where the tape is.)

4. Use the knitting needle or nail to make holes over the entire surface of the fruit, except where there is tape. Handle these sharp instruments carefully!

   There should be about 1/4 inch between holes. Less space than this makes the skin of the fruit too weak. However, too much space between holes is also a problem—the fruit will be more likely to rot.

   Each hole needs to be about twice as large as the stem of a clove. This keeps the cloves from falling out as the fruit dries and shrinks.

5. Once all of the holes have been made, remove the tape.

6. Press a whole clove firmly into each hole.

7. Pour the spice blend into the paper lunch bag. Place the pomander inside, and gently shake the bag until the pomander is completely covered with spices.

8. Roll the top of the bag to close it. Store the bag in a cupboard that is cool and dry. The remaining spices will be loose on the bottom of the bag.

9. Take out the bag once a day, and gently shake it to spread more spices over the pomander.

10. The pomander should be dry after about three weeks. If not, keep it in the bag, and check it daily.

11. Carefully shake the dry pomander to remove the extra spices from the surface. Tie a colorful ribbon around the once-taped space, making a bow at the top. Add a loop at the other end of the ribbon for hanging.

FIVE

Treating the Sick

A visit from the apothecary was rarely something to celebrate. Unless a baby was about to be born, his presence meant that someone in the house was sick. But colonial people were polite and proper. They greeted the apothecary with kindness, offering all the hospitality of their home. He knew that the family was worried and so stopped to greet them before seeing the patient.

What Ails You?

The apothecary treated plenty of injuries. He even performed surgery. When a bone was broken, the apothecary splinted it with a wooden box wrapped in bandages. He stitched up gashes and cut out infected tonsils. Infections could be treated with a technique called lancing. This involved piercing the skin with a sharp needle to let the fluids drain out. There was no reliable **anesthesia** available to numb the area during these procedures. Patients sometimes drank alcohol or took opium, a powerful drug made from poppy plants. Other plants used as anesthetics included mandrake, henbane, and nightshade. The apothecary had to be very careful with each dose. These plants could be deadly if misused.

Treating disease was more complicated. The apothecary could not always tell what caused a fever or see why a person was in pain. Even when he recognized the disease, the apothecary knew that medicines could not provide a miracle cure. His main goal was to make the patient feel better. To do this, he created a step-by-step plan. In the 1730s a typical plan to treat a cough looked like this:

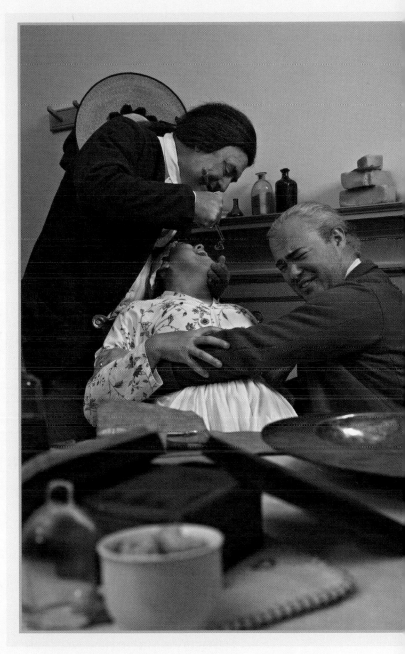

Along with making medicine, apothecaries performed surgical procedures when necessary.

It may be cured in the Beginning with riding moderately on Horseback every Day, and taking only a little Ground Ivy Tea sweeten'd with Syrrup of Horehound, at Night when you go to Bed. But in Case it be violent, it will be proper to bleed Eight Ounces, and . . . wash every Day in cold Water, and very often your Feet.

If the patient could walk, fresh air and exercise were always the first steps. Nature could then help speed the healing process. The apothecary also discussed diet. Most colonists ate meals heavy in meat and fat, with few vegetables. They drank ale and milk but considered water unsafe. And they loved sweets. The apothecary encouraged lighter meals when his patients were ill, often made with spices to encourage sweating, and herbal teas to drink.

Next the apothecary tried to ease the symptoms. Sometimes this was very effective. He prescribed calamine lotion for skin rashes. Willow bark, which contains the same chemical that is in aspirin, was used for headaches. Other treatments were far more dangerous. When a patient was very ill, the apothecary worked to restore balance to the bodily humors. Ipecac or castor oil was often given to cause vomiting and diarrhea. This treatment was supposed to improve patients' yellow and black bile. Instead, it often caused them to become weaker. Bloodletting was a common treatment

The apothecary did his best to treat his patients and make them feel better.

to reduce fever. If this failed, the apothecary might make a hot **poultice**. The poultice was a hot cloth containing acids or herbs that burned the patient's skin. A sore formed where the poultice was used. It oozed fluid, which was thought to be poison seeping from inside the body.

Colonial Americans took these miseries for granted. They gritted their teeth and bore the pain of treatment and healing, just as they tolerated all the hardships of their lives. The apothecary was not trying to hurt them. He was doing his best with age-old information and limited tools.

Stopping Disease

In the eighteenth century America's colonies were hit by one **epidemic** after another. Yellow fever and typhoid struck cities on the coast. Smallpox came to every town. It became clear that such diseases were contagious—they passed from person to person.

Boston had its seventh major smallpox outbreak in 1721 and 1722. Half of the people in Boston came down with a high fever and painful sores on their skin. About 15 percent of them died. Reverend Cotton Mather was a Boston minister and part-time apothecary. He had watched dozens of his neighbors die from smallpox. One day the reverend's slave, Onesimus, explained how he had been inoculated against smallpox as a child in Africa. Reverend Mather was excited by the idea and was willing to try anything to stop smallpox.

Mather contacted his friend Zabdiel Boylston, a Boston apothecary. Boylston agreed to try the procedure on 240 people, including his own family. He scratched each patient's skin and placed a small amount of smallpox pus into the wound. Other apothecaries thought this was a dangerous treatment and refused to try it. However, Dr. Boylston's experiment worked. Inoculated patients became slightly ill, but only about 2 percent died. After they recovered, these patients were immune to smallpox. They never got the disease again. Soon inoculation was used throughout the colonies.

Hospitals and Schools

Medical care took another step forward in 1751. That year Dr. Thomas Bond became inspired to open a hospital in Philadelphia. The city had grown rapidly. Dr. Bond wanted "to care for the sick-poor and insane who were wandering the streets of Philadelphia." He asked his friend Benjamin Franklin

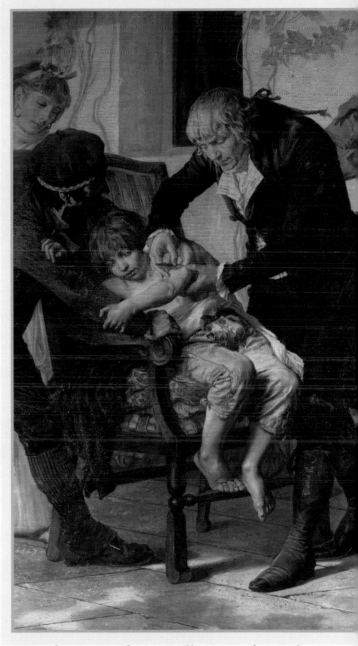

In order to combat smallpox in the early 1700s, patients were inoculated with pus.

Quarantine

Governments and doctors were desperate to stop the raging epidemics that swept through the colonies. They wondered if disease came from unclean air caused by animal waste and rotting vegetation. Colonists were also superstitious. Many suspected that disease was a punishment from God.

When medical experts began to look closely, they noticed a pattern. Epidemics often began after the arrival of ships. New York City began to quarantine ships in 1689. This kept them out of the harbor if any of their passengers were ill. In 1700 the governor of Pennsylvania passed a similar law, requiring infected ships to remain a mile offshore. Massachusetts officials decided to hold people responsible for bringing diseases to their colony. According to this law, ship captains or sick passengers were fined for the damage they caused.

to help. Franklin spoke to the Pennsylvania colonial government. He asked them to raise money for this cause. Some of the politicians were unhappy with the idea, but Franklin convinced them. Two years later Pennsylvania Hospital opened its doors. It not only helped Philadelphia's poor citizens. Doctors began to bring their

In 1753 Pennsylvania Hospital opened its doors to the sick.

apprentices on visits. This was a whole new way for them to learn.
The apprentices learned new skills on each visit, and they were
eager for more opportunities.

In 1765 the first colonial medical school opened its doors. The
University of Pennsylvania School of Medicine offered classes

in philosophy, plant biology, and other subjects. The school also required students to see patients at Pennsylvania Hospital. King's College in New York City soon offered a similar program.

However, change was slow. For many years the neighborhood apothecary shop remained a place where people looked for cures and comfort. The apothecary continued to make his rounds, birthing babies and saying a prayer for those he could not save.

Glossary

anesthesia	medicine given to relieve pain
apprentice	a person who learns a new skill or job by working with an expert
benefit	a medicine taken to prevent disease
bloodletting	drawing blood from the body to treat illness
compound	a medicine taken to treat illness, usually containing many ingredients
diagnosis	identifying an illness from its signs and symptoms
epidemic	a disease that spreads rapidly throughout a group of people
indenture	a contract between an apprentice and a master
master	an experienced craftsman or professional who trains apprentices
miasma	unclean air that was thought to carry disease
pharmacopoeia	a book of recipes for making medications
poultice	a moist cloth soaked in herbs and applied to the skin
preservative	a substance used to keep food from decaying
quarantine	to keep the sick separate from the healthy
simple	a medicine made from plants that is taken to treat illness
sundries	items other than medicines that are sold in an apothecary shop

Find Out More

BOOKS

Fradin, Brindell. *Jamestown, Virginia.* New York: Marshall Cavendish Benchmark, 2007.

Kalman, Bobbie. *A Visual Dictionary of a Colonial Community.* New York: Crabtree Publishing Company, 2008.

Mara, Wil. *The Farmer.* New York: Marshall Cavendish Benchmark, 2010.

McNeese, Tim. *Williamsburg.* New York: Chelsea House Publications, 2007.

Roberts, Russell. *Life in Colonial America.* Hockessin, DE: Mitchell Lane Publishers, 2007.

Ruby, Lois. *Journey to Jamestown.* Boston: Kingfisher, 2005.

WEBSITES

Colonial Apothecary

www.history.org/almanack/life/trades/tradeapo.cfm

The Colonial Williamsburg website offers a closer look at the work of an apothecary.

Colonial Williamsburg Kids' Zone

www.history.org/kids/

Tour the colonial capital of Virginia and meet some of its important residents. There are games and activities, as well as many resources about colonial life and history.

Jamestown Online Adventure

www.historyglobe.com/jamestown/

This interactive website allows you to build a colony at Jamestown. See if you can survive the challenges of life in seventeenth-century America!

Index

Page numbers in **boldface** are illustrations.

pharmacopoeia, 21

Pennsylvania Hospital, 40–42, **41**

physicians, 7

plantations, 13

poultice, 37

quarantine, 40

religious freedom, 9

Robertson, Andrew, 23

schools, 39–42

shops, apothecary, 11–12, 24, **25,** 26–30

simples, 28

sundries, 26

surgeons, 6–8

treatments, 34–42

University of Pennsylvania School of Medicine, 41–42

villages, 12–13

Virginia Company of London, 6

About the Author

Christine Petersen is a freelance writer and environmental educator who lives near Minneapolis, Minnesota. A former middle school teacher, she has written more than three dozen books for young people that cover a wide range of topics in social studies and science. When she's not writing, Petersen conducts naturalist programs and spends time with her young son. She is a member of the Society of Children's Book Writers and Illustrators.